THE FUTURE FOOTBALL STAR

Written and Illustrated by Kim Ruff-Moore

Copyright Page
The Future Football Star
Written and Illustrated by Kim Ruff Moore
Cover Design by Kim Ruff Moore
Copyright © 2025 by Kim Ruff Moore
All rights reserved. No part of this publication may be reproduced, stored in a retrieval system, or transmitted in any form or by any means—electronic, mechanical, photocopying, recording, or otherwise—without prior written permission from the publisher.
Published by Ruff Moore Media
Printed in the United States of America
For more information, visit:
www.kimruffmoore.com
ISBN: 9798306628899

To every child with big dreams,
may you run boldly toward your future,
knowing that greatness is within you.
And to my family and community,
thank you for always cheering me on.

Other Children's Books:
Suzzie Mocha Series
Pebo Pig Series
Sergio the Mouse Series
Otis the Brown Bear
Spence Seven Series
Land of Unicorns Series
I Want to Sing Like Whitney
Bria Gets New Braids
Klohe's Favorite Things
Oliver and the Ocean
Love Brought Max Home
A Horse Called Midnight
Mommy, I Can Do It Series
Faus the Fox Finds Fall Colors
Elo the Elephant Forgets Everything
And Many More!

In a small Southern town, a little boy named Nate loved football more than anything. With a ball always in his hand, he ran through the fields like the wind.

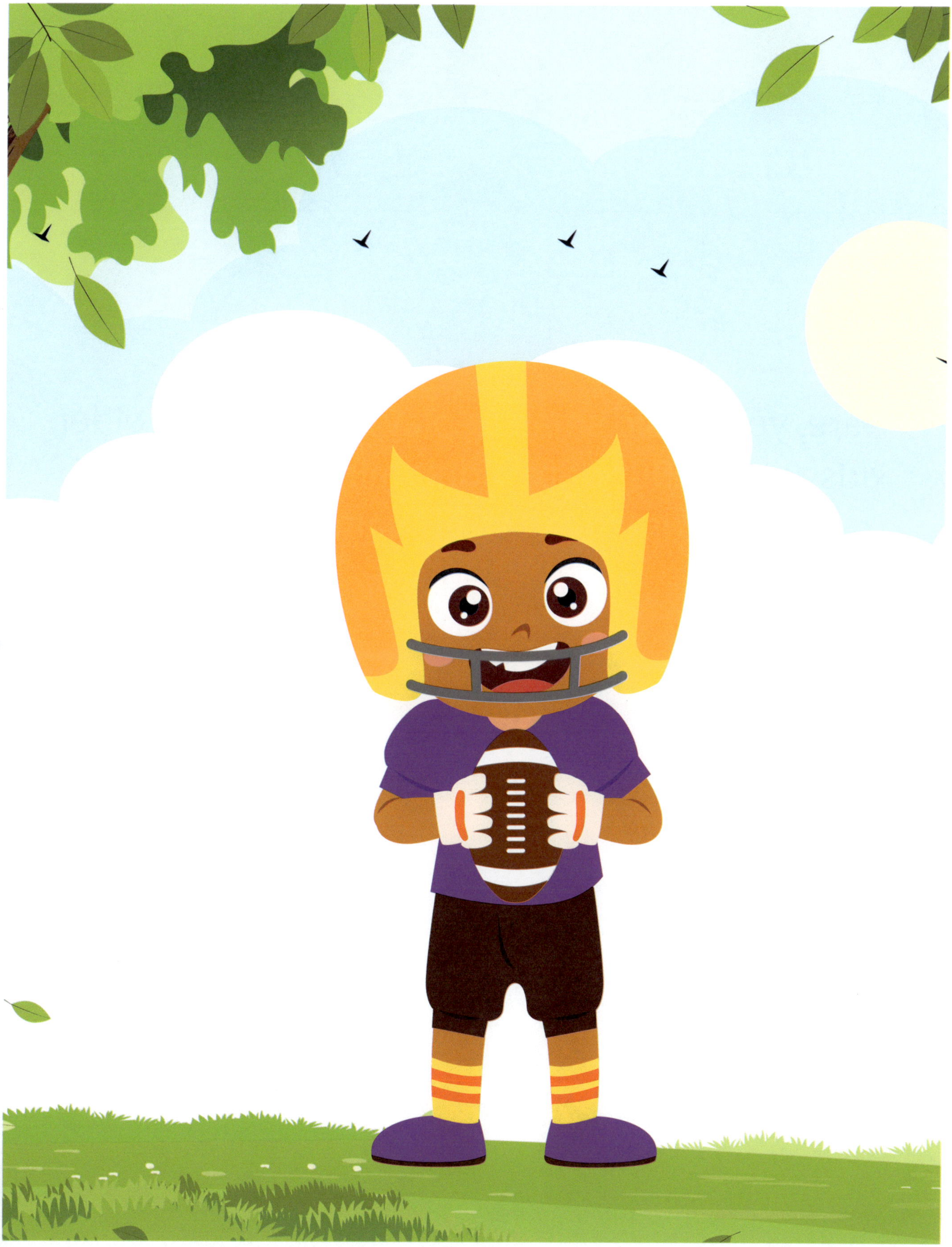

"Nate, you're too small to play with us!" the older kids teased. But Nate didn't mind. He practiced every day, dreaming of big games and roaring crowds.

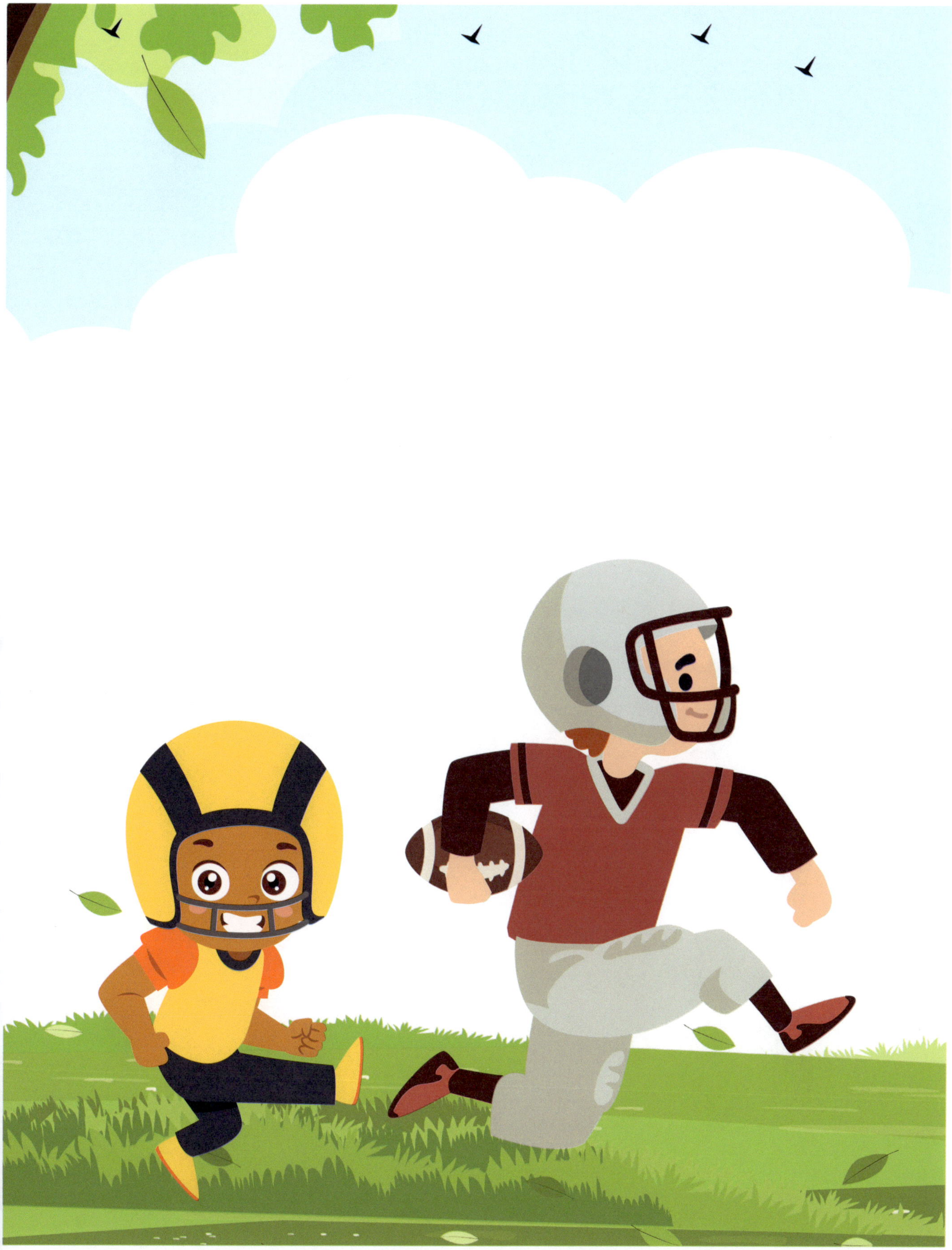

In the backyard, Nate's grandpa set up cones for him to run around. "Greatness starts with hard work," Grandpa said. "And you've got the heart, boy."

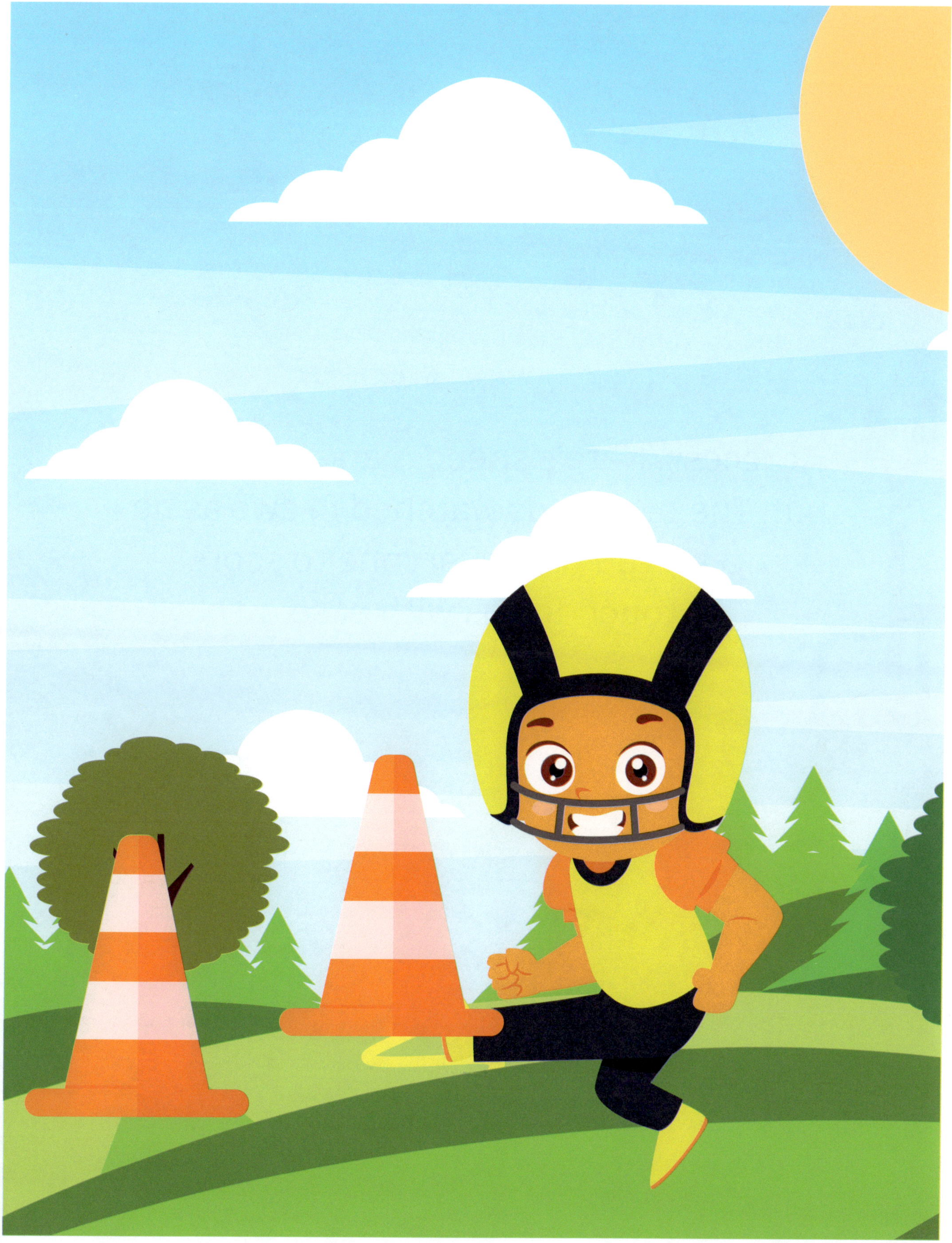

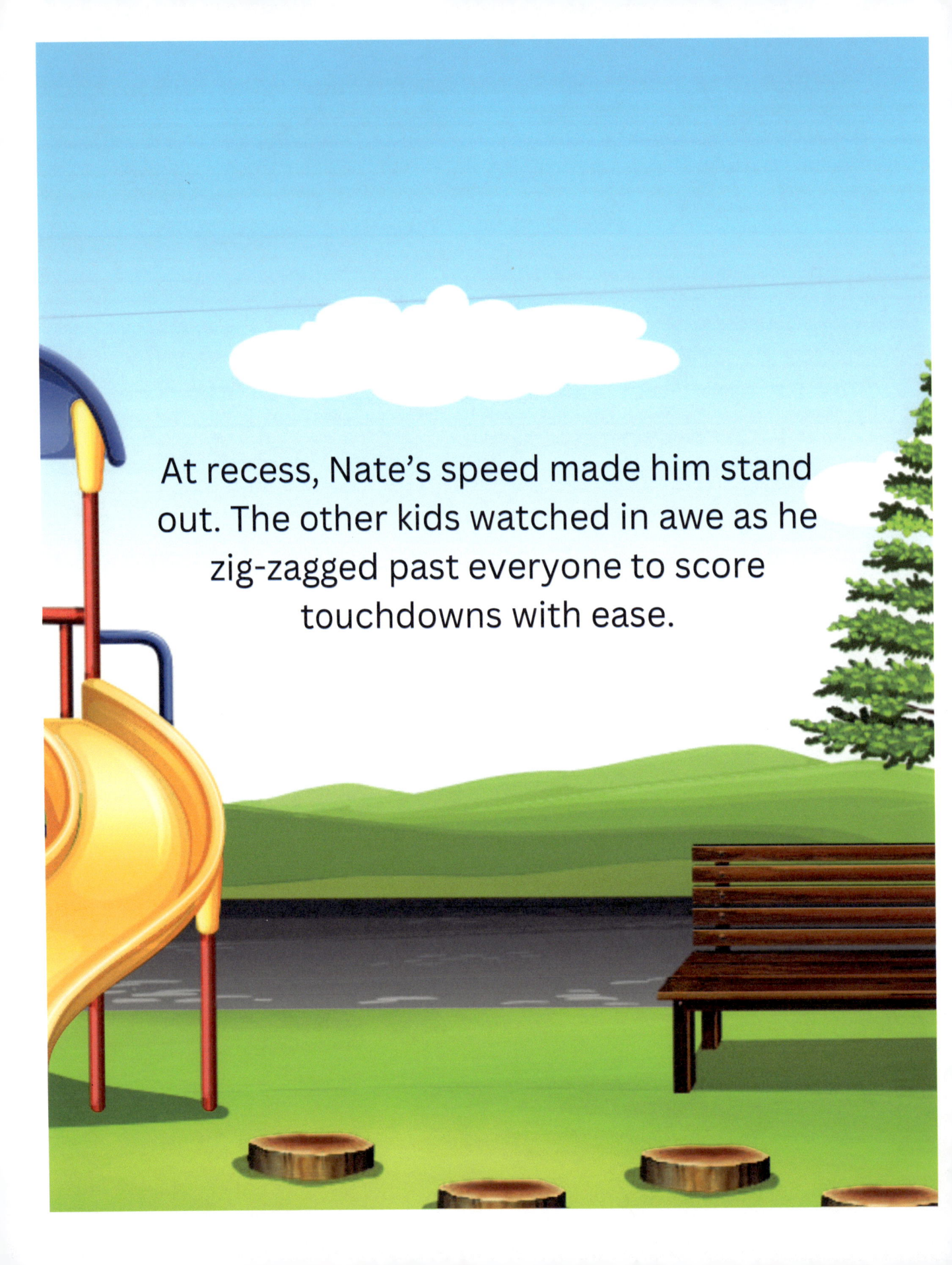

At recess, Nate's speed made him stand out. The other kids watched in awe as he zig-zagged past everyone to score touchdowns with ease.

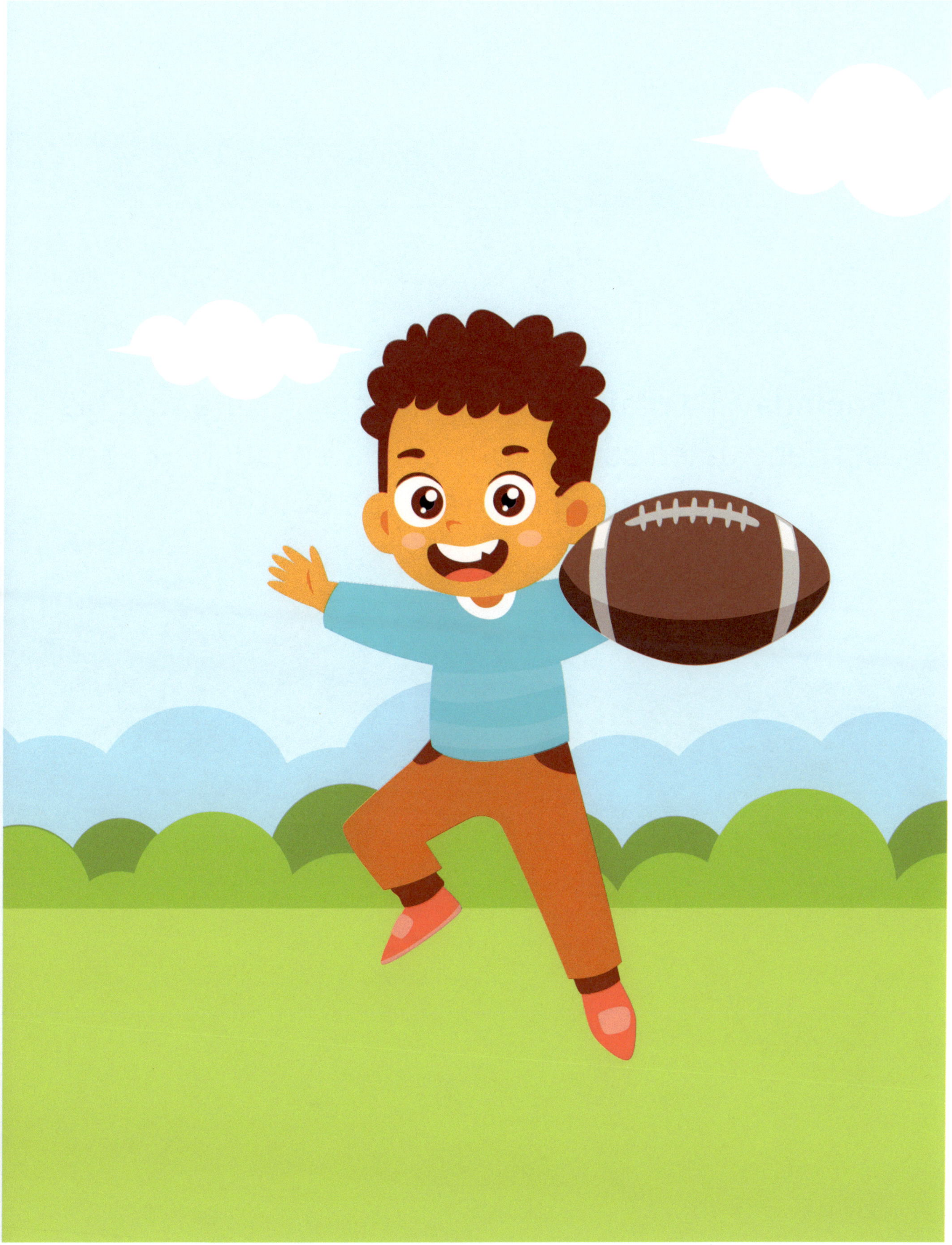

"Someday, I'll play in the big leagues," Nate told his best friend Jalen as they played. Jalen laughed. "You? You're just a kid from the South!"

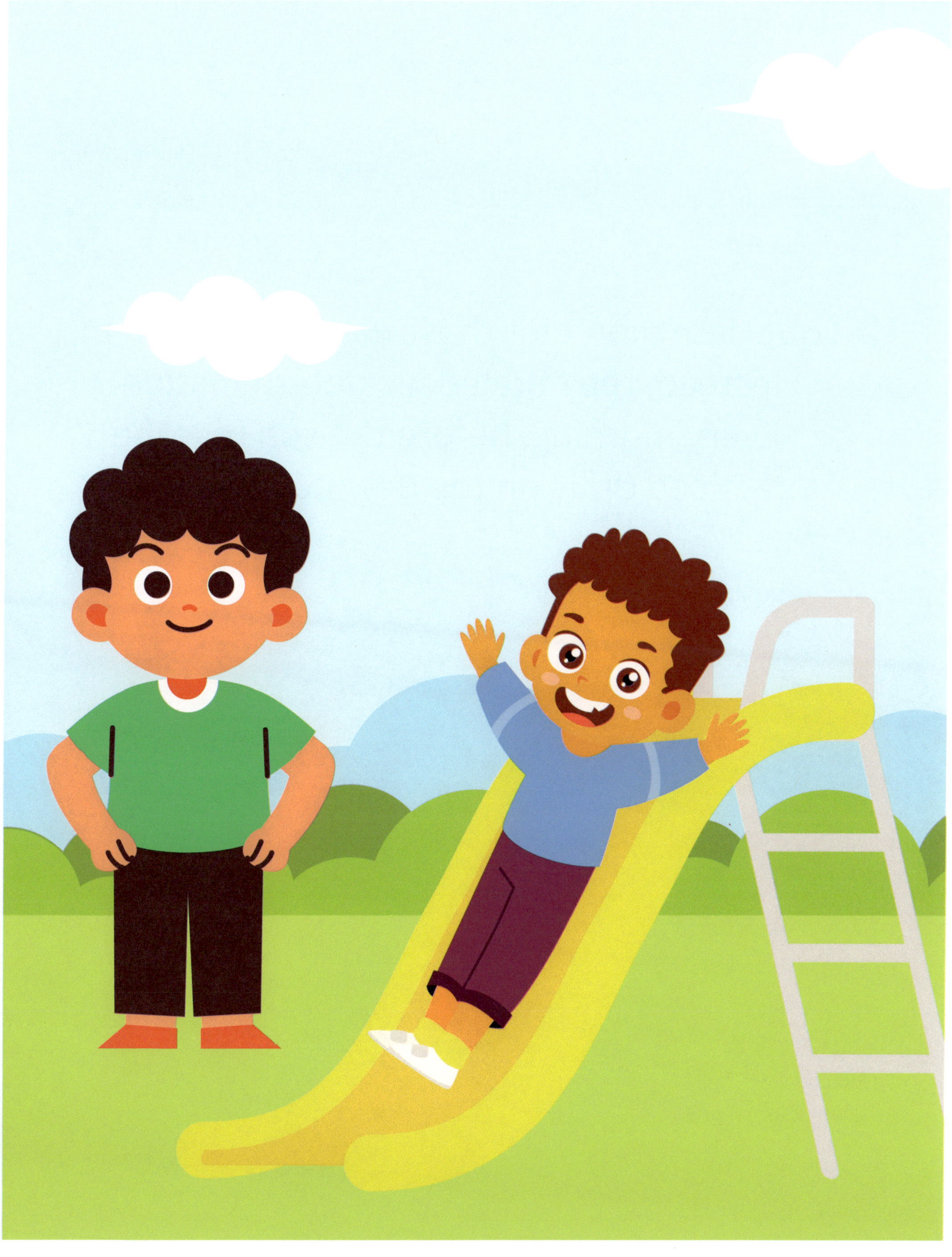

But Nate didn't let those words bother him. Instead, they fueled his determination. Every morning, before the sun rose, he practiced drills on the dew-covered grass.

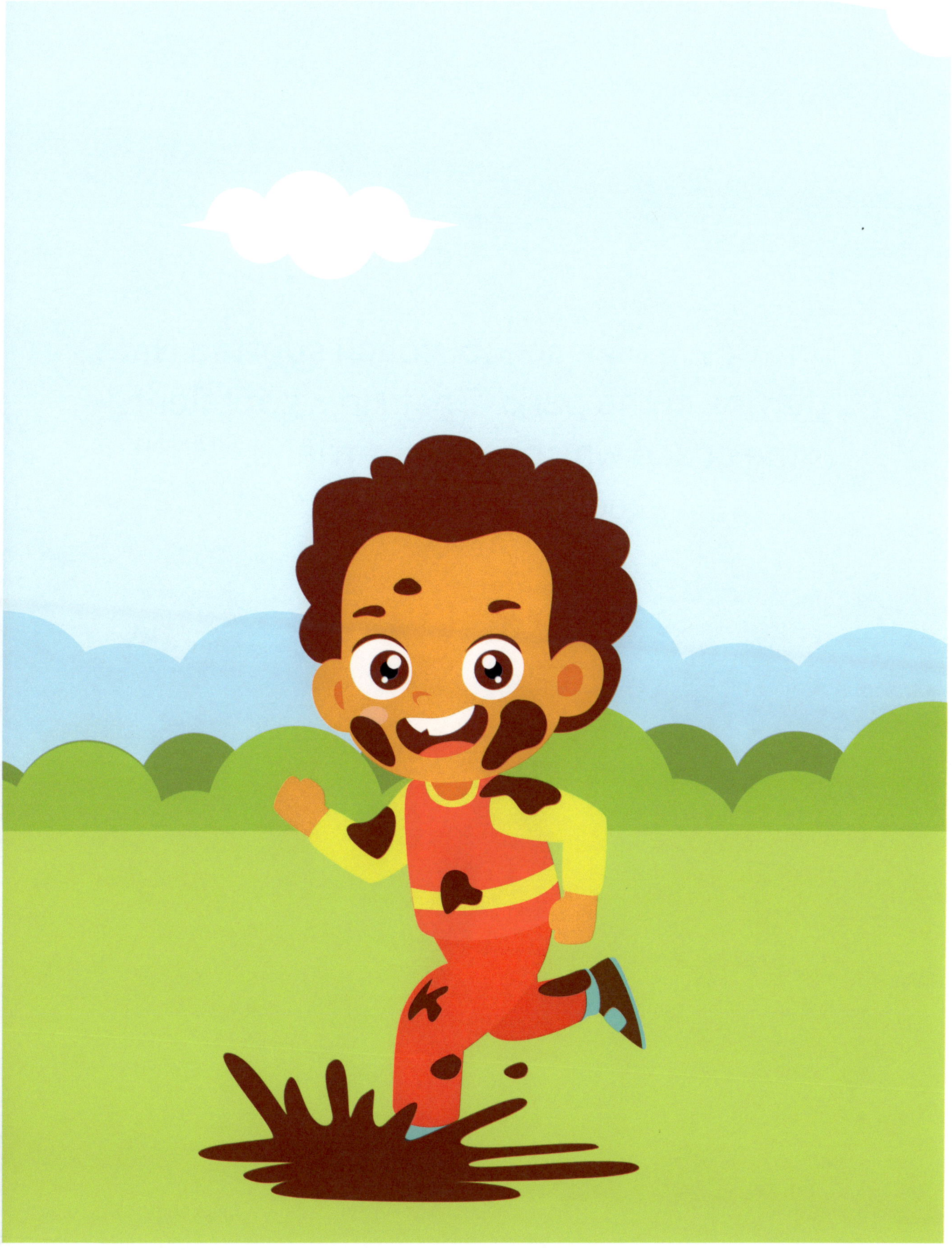

One day, a high school coach spotted Nate playing in the park. "That kid's got talent," the coach whispered to a friend. "We'll keep an eye on him."

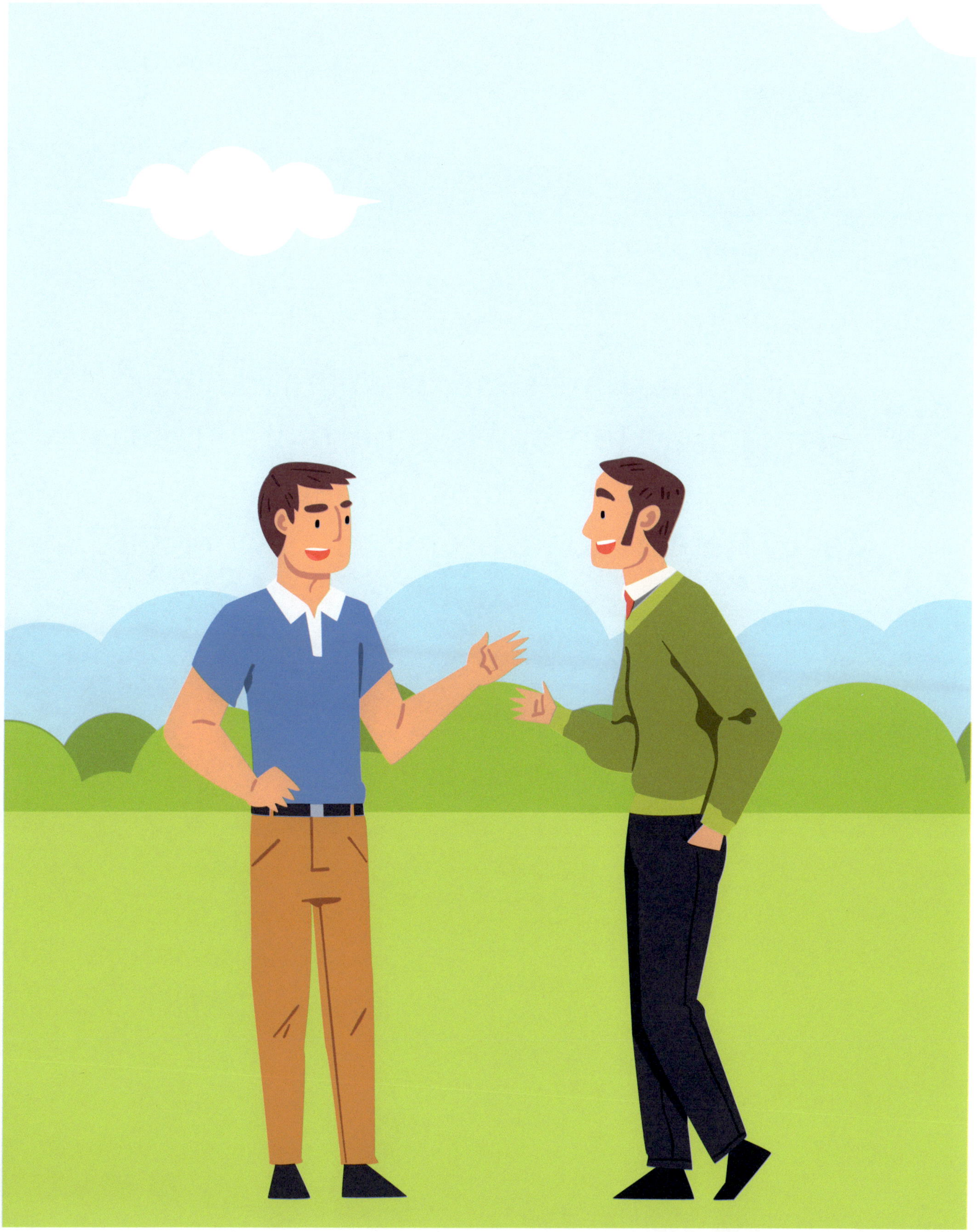

At home, Nate's mom reminded him, "Remember, football is important, but so is school. Use your mind as much as your feet." Nate nodded, promising to work hard at both.

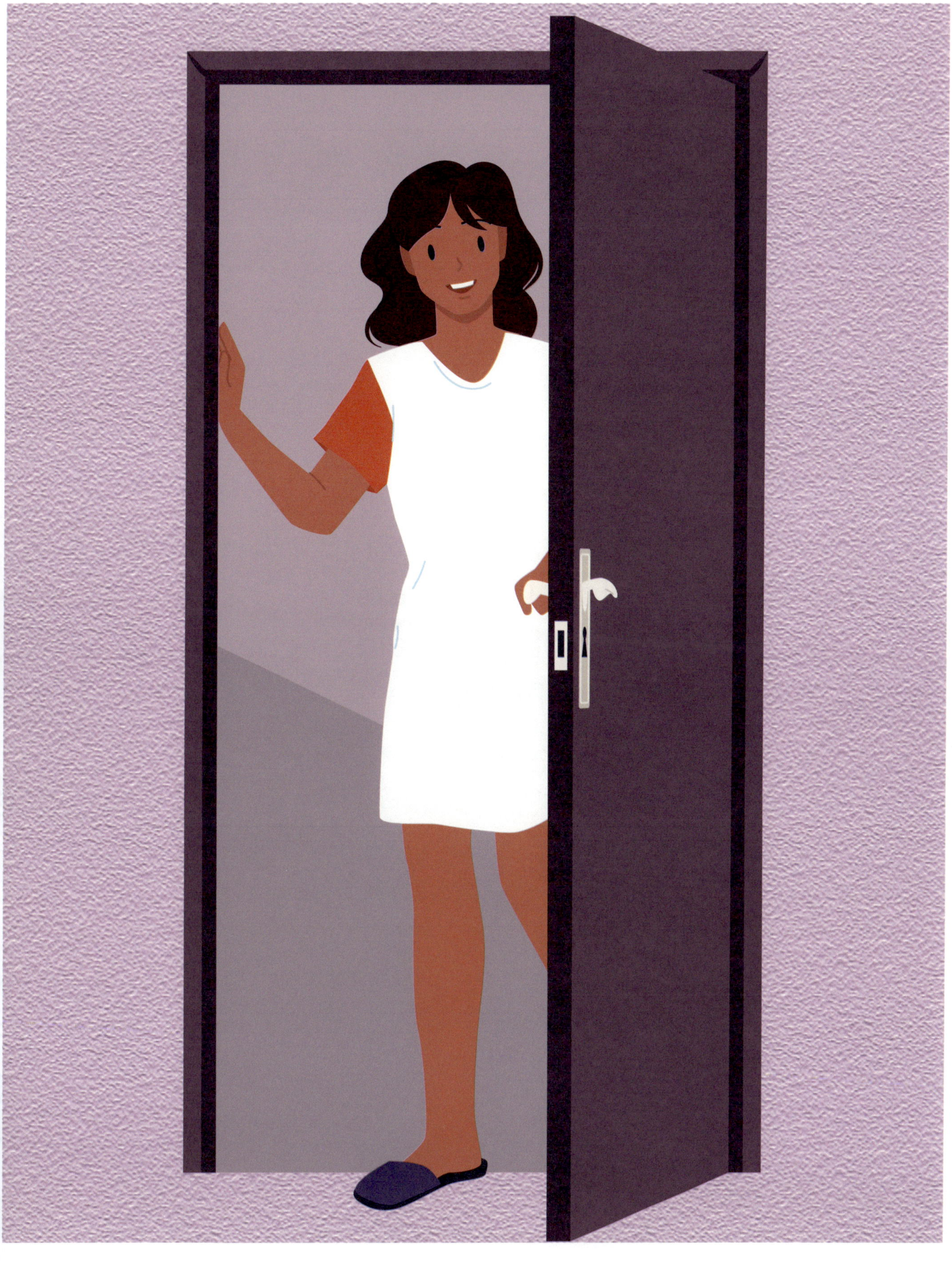

By middle school, Nate's name was already buzzing in the local community. "That boy's got something special," said the barber at the shop.

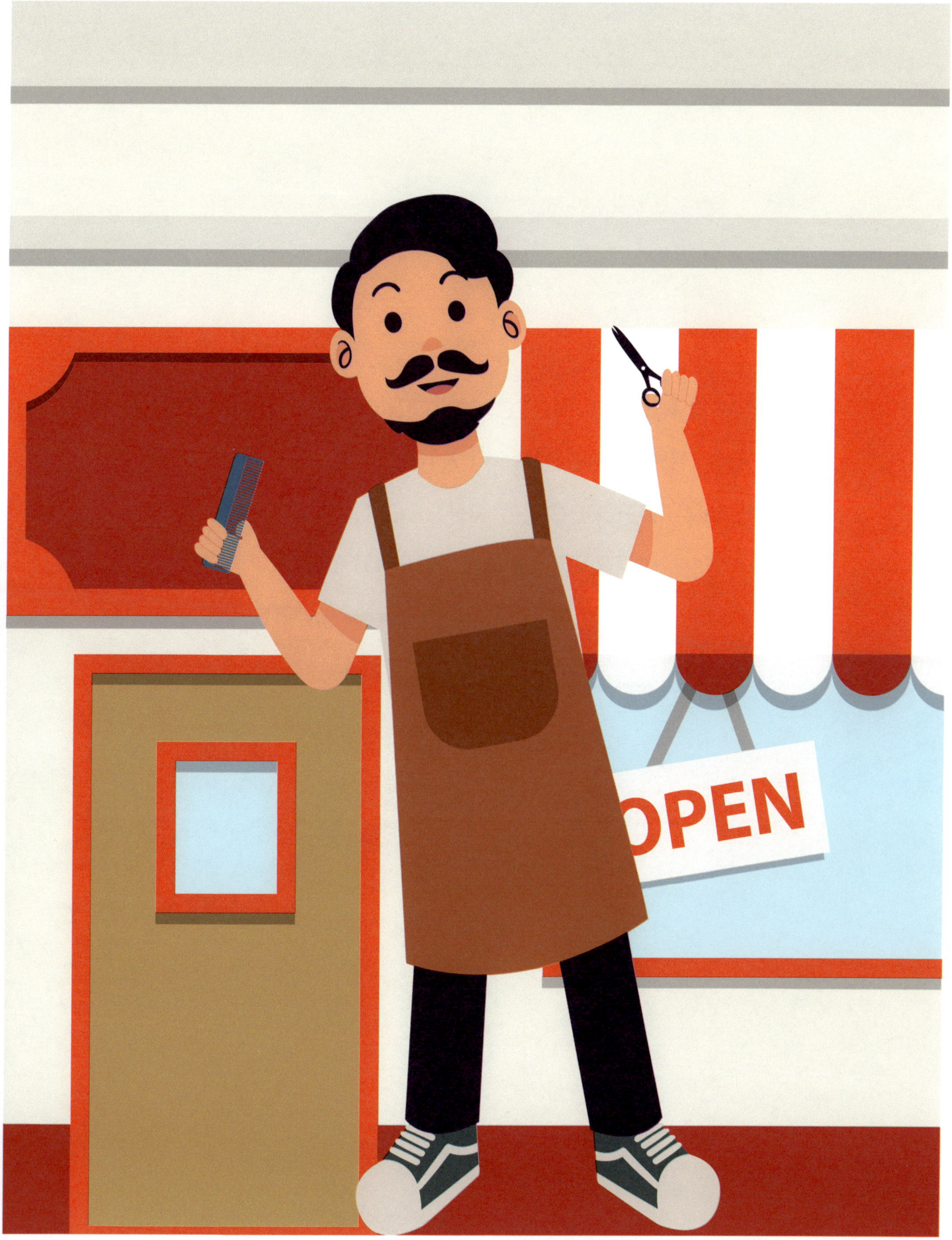
OPEN

Even when Nate got tired, he thought about his dreams. "One day, I'll be on TV," he whispered to himself. "One day, I'll make Grandpa proud."

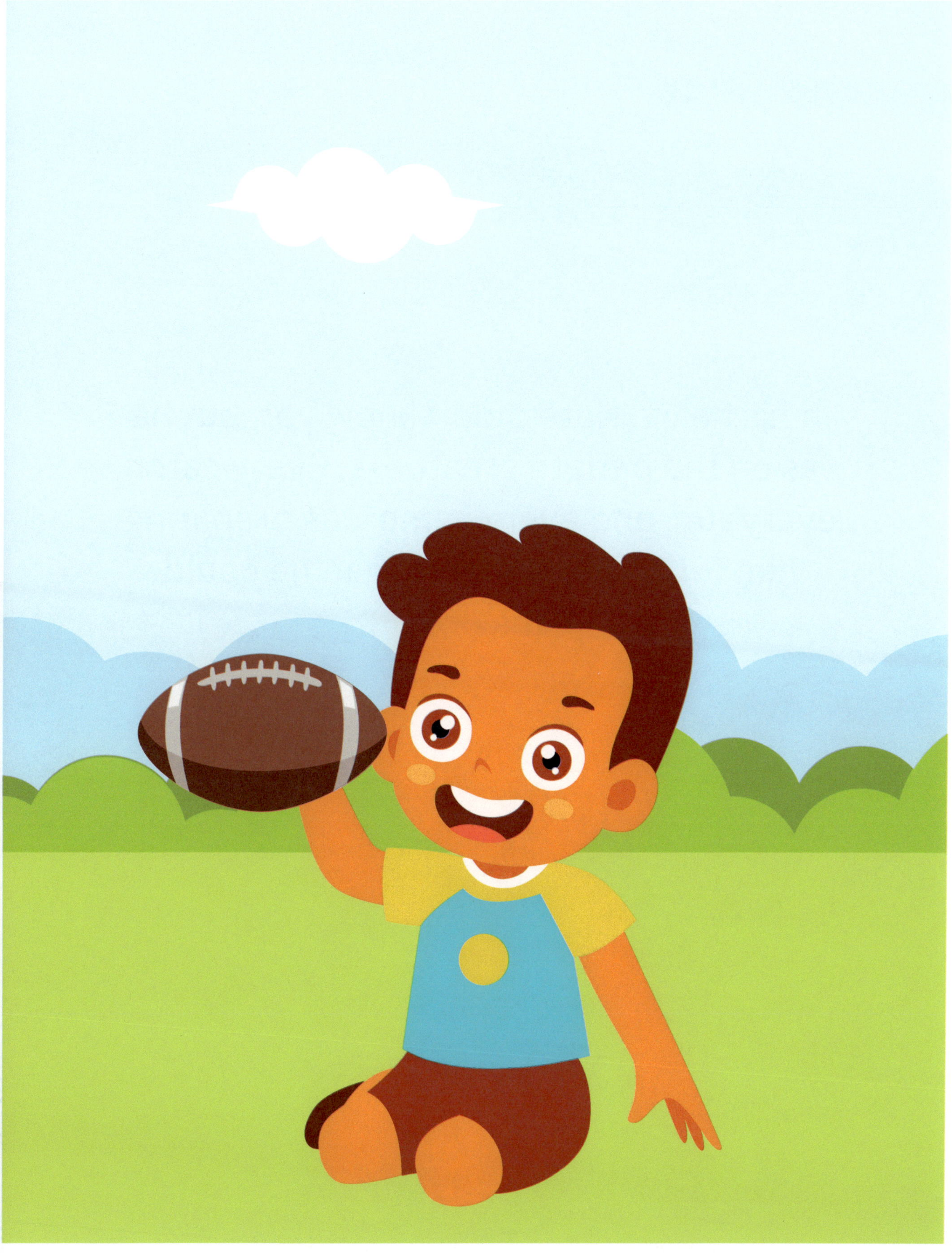

In his heart, Nate didn't know yet, but he was on the path to greatness. Every catch, every run, and every game was preparing him for a future bigger than he could imagine.

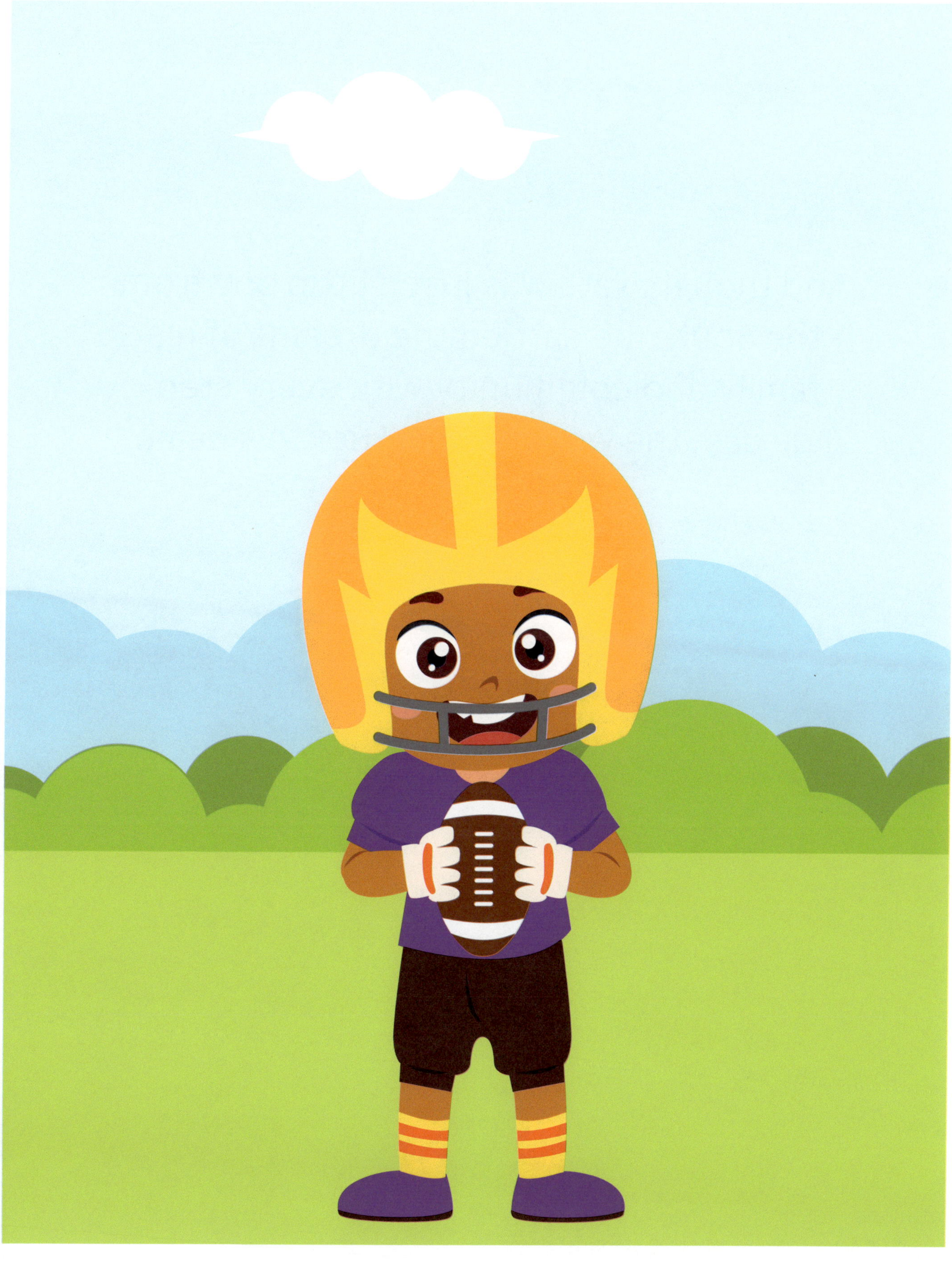

And though Nate was just a little boy from the South, he carried the dreams of his family and community with every step. One day, the world would know his name.

Epilogue: Nate's Next Chapter

The roar of the crowd was deafening as Nate stood on the field, helmet in hand, staring up at the scoreboard. His team had just secured the state championship, and for a moment, time seemed to freeze. All the early mornings, late-night practices, and the sacrifices he and his family made were worth it. Nate smiled, not just because of the win, but because this moment was a testament to perseverance, grit, and faith.

As the confetti rained down, Nate thought back to his small-town beginnings—the backyard football games, the endless drills his dad ran with him, and the teachers and coaches who never let him settle for less than his best. Their belief in him was the foundation of his journey. Though the championship was a milestone, Nate knew it was only the beginning. He had dreams of playing college football, walking across that stage at the NFL draft, and using his platform to inspire others. He wanted to be more than just a player—he wanted to be a leader, a role model, and a voice for kids who dared to dream big.

As he raised the trophy high above his head, Nate whispered a promise to himself: "This is for everyone who believed in me—and for those who need someone to believe in them."

The future football star had arrived, but his greatest victories were still ahead.

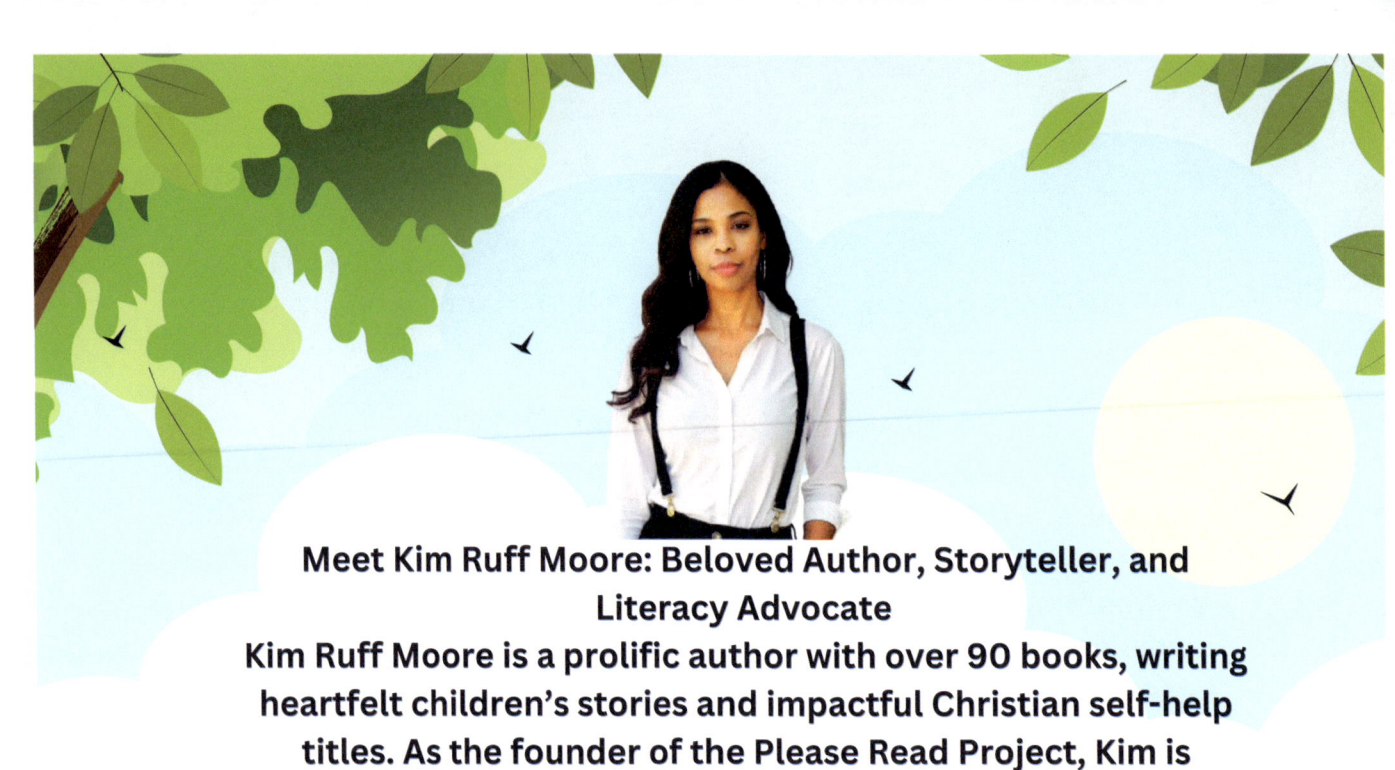

Meet Kim Ruff Moore: Beloved Author, Storyteller, and Literacy Advocate

Kim Ruff Moore is a prolific author with over 90 books, writing heartfelt children's stories and impactful Christian self-help titles. As the founder of the Please Read Project, Kim is dedicated to promoting literacy, donating her books to children and adults who need them most. Her diverse catalog of children's books, including favorites like the Pebo Pig Prefers and Suzzie Mocha series, brings joy and imagination to readers of all ages. Among her inspiring adult works are I Still Have Joy, Never Put All Your Eggs in One Basket, Waymaker, and Girl Mash the Gas.

Kim's books are widely available at Walmart, Barnes & Noble, Books-A-Million, Harvard Book Store, and other major retailers. Beyond writing, she's a Stellar Award-winning singer-songwriter and a member of The New Consolers with her husband, Jeffery Moore.

Discover more about Kim's work at kimruffmoore.com and ruffmooremedia.com.

Made in the USA
Columbia, SC
14 February 2025